Read Me First

- Descriptions in this manual are based at the time of writing this guide, and it may not be 100% accurate again if there is a major software update to All-New Echo Dot (3rd Generation).

- All information supplied in this guide is for educational purpose only and users bear the responsibility for using it.

- Although I took tremendous effort to ensure that all information provided in this guide are correct, I will welcome your suggestions if you find out that any information provided in this guide is inadequate or you find a better way of doing some of the actions mentioned in this guide. All correspondence should be sent to pharmibrahimguides@gmail.com

Copyright and Trademarks

Echo Dot is a trademark of Amazon, Inc. All other trademarks are the property of their respective owners. Reproduction of this book without the permission of the owner is illegal. Any request for permission should be directed to **pharmibrahimguides@gmail.com**.

Copyright © 2018 by Pharm Ibrahim

About This Guide

Finally, a concise, straightforward and succinct manual on All-New Echo Dot (3rd Generation) for newbies, seniors, students, instructors and tech lovers is here. This is the guide Amazon should have included in the box.

I know you have a lot of things to do and you will not want to be bothered by irrelevant things, so I have made this manual to be very concise and straightforward. Interestingly, it is a step-by-step manual, so you can be confident that you will understand the information contained inside it.

PS: Please make sure you don't give the gift of All-New Echo Dot (3rd Generation) without given this companion guide alongside with it. This guide makes your gift a complete one.

Table of Contents

How to Use This Guide — vi

Introduction — 1

Unpacking Your Device — 1

Get to know your device — 1

    Get to Know the Buttons on Echo Dot — *1*

Different Light Ring Statuses — 2

Turning your Echo Dot On and Off — 4

Getting started with Echo Dot — 4

    Troubleshooting Wi-Fi Connection When Using Alexa App or Echo Dot — 9

Connecting Echo Dot to a Wi-Fi/Mobile Hotspot — 10

Change the Wake Word — 12

Connecting Echo Dot to Bluetooth Devices — 14

    Connecting Echo Dot to a Mobile Bluetooth Device — *15*

    Connecting Echo Dot to a Bluetooth Speaker — *17*

Using Echo Dot with IFTTT — 19

Using Echo Dot with Different Types of Skills — 21

Connecting Your Smart Devices to Echo Dot — 23

    Grouping Your Smart Home Devices — 26

Troubleshooting Skills — 27

Communicating with Echo Dot 29

    Speaking to Echo Dot 29

    Getting What You Want from Echo Dot 29

    Using Echo Dot with Smart Home Devices 30

    Using Quick Commands (Routines) to Manage Echo Dot Like a Pro 31

    Using Echo Dot with Your Calendar 35

    Using Echo Dot with Your Shopping List and To-do List 37

    Using Echo Dot with Alarm 38

    Using Echo Dot with Timer 42

    Using Echo Dot with Clock 44

    Using Echo Dot to Get Flight Information 44

    Listen to Your Audiobooks 45

    Read Kindle Books with Alexa 46

    Buying Items Using Your Voice 47

    Using Echo Dot to Get Traffic Information 48

    What about Math? 49

    Using Echo Dot to get definitions 49

    Using Echo Dot with Wikipedia 49

    Using Echo to Listen to Radio Programs 49

    Using Echo Dot to Get Flash Briefing 50

    Using Echo Dot to Get General Information 51

    Using Echo Dot to Make an Announcements or Broadcast 51

    Funny sides of Echo Dot 52

Calling and Messaging on Echo Dot 54

    Using Do Not Disturb 57

Echo Dot's Settings 59

    Clearing your voice input and interactions 59

Troubleshooting Echo Dot 60

Resetting Echo Dot	61
Bonus Chapter –Being Productive with Echo Dot	62
Starting Your Day with Echo Dot	*62*
Reviewing Your Day with Echo Dot	*63*
Just Before You Go... (Please Read!)	64

How to Use This Guide

This guide is an unofficial manual of All-New Echo Dot (3rd Generation) and it should be used just like you use any reference book or manual.

To quickly find a topic, please use the table of contents. In addition, you can press **Ctrl** + **F** if you are using a PC, if not press the menu icon (usually located at the right top corner of the screen) of your reading app and select "**Search**" to search for any phrase in this guide. Also, you can simply search for word/phrase by tapping on the search icon (the lens icon) usually located at the top of the screen. Searching for keywords or phrase will allow you to quickly find information and save time.

You don't need to stick to commands given in this manual. In fact, you could probably say all the example commands given in this guide in another ways; the most important thing is to get Echo Dot to understand what you are saying.

Lastly, I have based the descriptions in this manual on the assumption that you will be controlling your Echo Dot using the wake word "Alexa". However, if you are using another wake word, you can get the same result just by replacing "Alexa" with the wake word you are using.

I hope this guide helps you get the most out of your Echo Dot.

Introduction

Echo Dot is a low price, but functionally similar version of Amazon Echo. Echo Dot is about 1.7 inches tall making it slightly taller than the second-generation Echo Dot. This guide will show you how to manage Echo Dot like a pro and how to ask questions and give commands that Echo Dot will understand.

Unpacking Your Device

When you unpack your product box, check your product box for the following items:
1. Echo Dot
2. Power adapter (15W)
3. Quick Start Guide

Get to know your device

Get to Know the Buttons on Echo Dot

Button	Function
⊕	Volume Up Button

	Action Button: This button can be used to wake your device, turn off a timer or alarm and enable Wi-Fi setup mode. To use the Action button to enable Wi-Fi mode press and hold it for about five seconds.
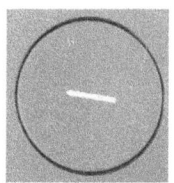	Volume Down Button
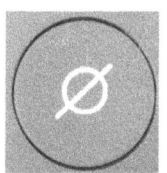	Microphone Button: Press this button to turn off the microphones. When this microphone is off, the light ring turns red and Echo Dot will not respond to your voice requests. To turn on the microphone again, press this button again. **Tip**: When you are going out of your home and you don't want Echo Dot to respond to people, just turn off the microphones by pressing the Microphone button. To begin to use the Echo Dot again, press microphone button again.

Different Light Ring Statuses

Light ring tells you many things about your device.
1. When the light ring is not showing any light (but it is connected to a power source), then your device is active and waiting for your request.

2. Orange light rotating clockwise means your device is connecting to a Wi-Fi network.
3. Solid blue with cyan pointing in direction of person speaking means Alexa is busy processing your request.
4. Solid blue with rotating cyan lights means your device is starting up.
5. Alternating solid blue and cyan lights means your device is responding.
6. Solid red light means the microphones on your device is turned off.
7. White light means you are changing the volume level on your device.
8. Continuous pulsing violet light means that an error occurred during the Wi-Fi setup of your Echo Dot.
9. A single flash of purple light after you have interacted with Alexa means that Do Not Disturbed is enabled. To learn more about Do Not Disturb, please go to page 57.
10. A green light moving clockwise means that a call is currently active on your device.
11. A pulsing green light (a green light appearing and disappearing) means that you are receiving a call.
12. A pulsing yellow light (a yellow light appearing and disappearing) means that you have a message or notification. To learn more about messaging, please go to page 56.

Turning your Echo Dot On and Off

Just like many other smart devices, turning on your device is as simple as ABC. To turn on your Echo Dot, just connect it to a power output using the power adapter that came with it. The light ring on Echo Dot turns on and after few seconds, Alexa lets you know that it is ready for setup. Please note that you might need to remove the protective nylon before you connect for the first time.

Please note that you may not get your Echo Dot to work using just any charger. I would advise that you always connect your Echo Dot to a power outlet using the power adapter that came with it.

To turn off Echo Dot, unplug it from the power source.

Tip: Amazon recommends that place your Echo Dot at least 20cm or eight inches from any walls or objects.

Getting started with Echo Dot

You will need to setup Echo Dot when you first start using it and you will learn how to do that in this section of the guide. To setup Echo Dot you will need the following things:

1. Echo Dot
2. Internet Access through a Wi-Fi Network.
3. A tablet or phone with Alexa app.

Alexa app is free and you can download it from the Google Play Store, Amazon App Store or Apple App Store. All you need to do is to go to one of this app store, search for **Amazon Alexa App** and tap the download button. Then tap Begin Setup and follow the prompts.

To setup Echo Dot:

1. Connect Echo Dot to a power output using the power adapter that came with it. Echo Dot then light up automatically. After some seconds, Alexa greets you and lets you know that it is ready for setup.
   Tip: If you have more than one Alexa devices, place them in separate rooms for optimum results.
2. Open Alexa app. I assumed you have installed Alexa app following the instructions above. For the purpose of discussion, I will assume that you are controlling/setting up your Echo Dot using the Alexa app installed on your tablet or phone.
3. In the Alexa app, sign in using your Amazon account details (if needed). If you are using the app for the first time, tap **Get Started** and follow the prompts.
4. Tap the menu button ☰ located at the top left corner of the screen, then tap **Alexa Devices**. If you are using Fire tablet, you can access the menu by swiping in from the left edge of the screen.

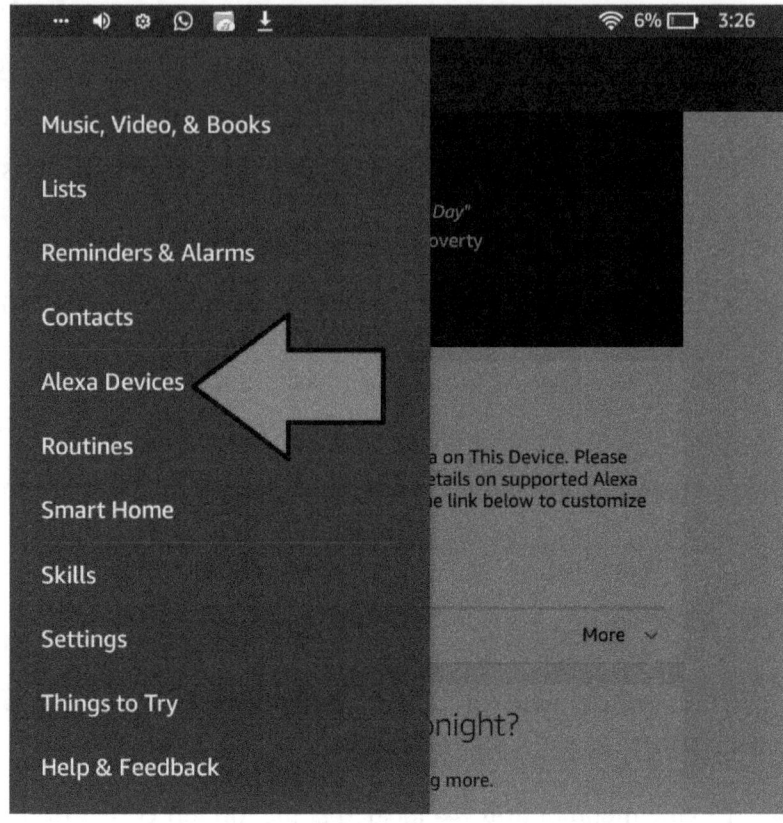

5. Tap **Add Alexa Device** and carefully follow the prompts.

Tip: If you are using Kindle Fire and you can't connect to Wi-Fi, do the following:

a) Go to Wi-Fi settings on your Fire tablet and select the network of the format **Amazon-FXX**.
b) On the Alexa app screen, tap **Continue**.

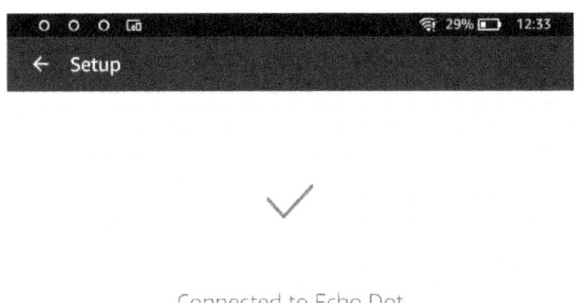

c) A list of available Wi-Fi networks then appears, tap on a Wi-Fi network. Enter a password for the network and tap on **Connect/Join** (if necessary). If you don't see your network, tap **Rescan**.

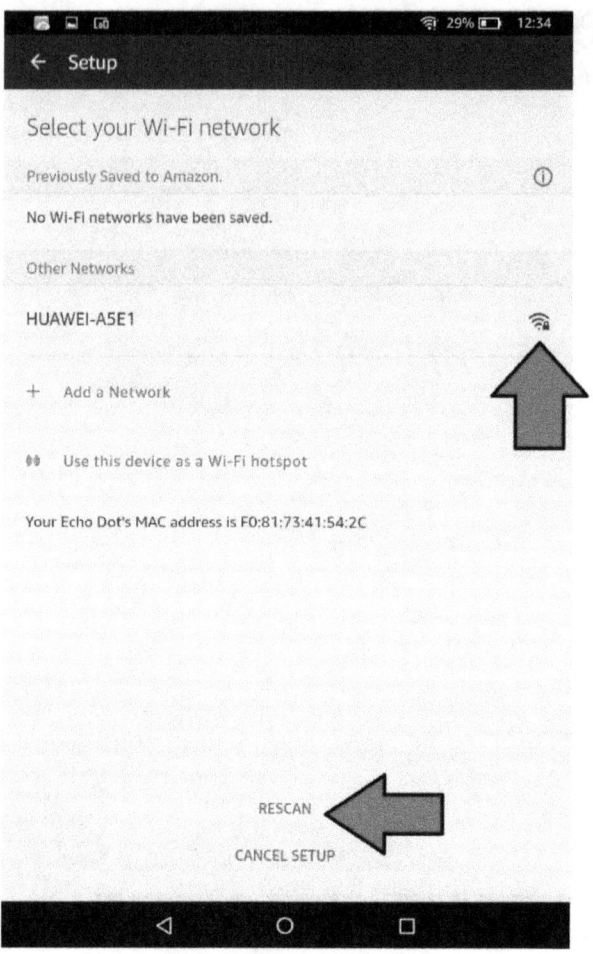

d) Then wait for the Echo Dot to connect to a Wi-Fi network. After your device connects to your Wi-Fi network, a confirmation message appears in the app. Tap **Continue** to allow your Echo Dot to perform a system update (if necessary).

You can perform many tweaks on Echo Dot using the Alexa App. More on this in the latter parts if this book.

Tip: You can follow similar steps mentioned above to update your Wi-Fi network on Echo Dot. Simply follow steps 1 to 4 above and tap **Echo Dot.** Tap **Change** next to **Wi-Fi Network** and follow the prompts.

Note: If you see a continuous pulsing violet light during the Echo Dot setup, then there is an error during the Wi-Fi setup of your Echo Dot. To rectify this, simply disconnect the Echo Dot from the power source and reconnect it again. Thereafter, repeat the steps 1 to 5 above.

Troubleshooting Wi-Fi Connection When Using Alexa App or Echo Dot

Echo Dot or Alexa App may sometimes refuse to process your request or connect the Wi-Fi network. When this happens, you may try any or some of the suggestions below:

Make sure you don't have limited network connectivity in that area. If your network is good and you still cannot connect, you may perform any of these actions.

- Try restarting the Wi-Fi.
- Move closer to your router and scan for the available networks. If the network still does not show up, you may add the network manually.
- Restart your router and modem. Unplug the modem and router for few minutes and plug the modem in, then the router.

- Unplug your Echo Dot from the power source, wait for few seconds and plug it back.
- If your phone/tablet is not connecting to the internet, make sure the Flight Mode is off. To check whether Flight mode is enabled, swipe down from the top of the screen if you are using an Android or Fire OS, flight mode icon ✈ will appear bold when enabled/on. Please note that the flight mode should be disabled/off to access wireless networks.
- Try restarting you phone/tablet.
- Try to contact your network service provider for further assistance if the suggestions above do not work.

Connecting Echo Dot to a Wi-Fi/Mobile Hotspot

For one reason or the other you may want to use your phone as a hotspot and connect your Echo Dot to it. Doing this is quite simple and it is discussed below:

1. Turn on the hotspot feature on your phone. Please refer to your phone's manual if you don't know how to activate this feature. In addition, please note that you may incur some extra charges while using your phone as a hotspot.
2. While the Echo Dot is connected to a power source and working, open the Alexa app on your mobile device.

3. In the Alexa app, tap the menu button ☰ located at the top left corner of the screen and tap **Alexa devices**. If you are using Fire tablet, you can access the menu by swiping in from the left edge of the screen.
4. If you are changing the Wi-Fi network, select your device **(Echo Dot)** from the list, select **Change** next to **Wi-Fi Network** and follow the prompts. If you are not changing the Wi-Fi network but registering a wireless network for the first time, tap **Add Alexa Device**, select **Echo Dot** and follow the prompts.
5. The ling ring on your device should turn orange when it is ready to connect to a Wi-Fi. If this does not happen, press the action button (the small dot icon on your Echo Dot).
6. A list of available Wi-Fi networks then appears in the app, tap the name of a network corresponding to your mobile hotspot, enter the password and tap **Connect** and wait for the connection to be established.
7. If you can't see the name of your mobile hotspot, scroll down on the Alexa app and select **Use this device as a Wi-Fi hotspot**. Then follow the prompts.

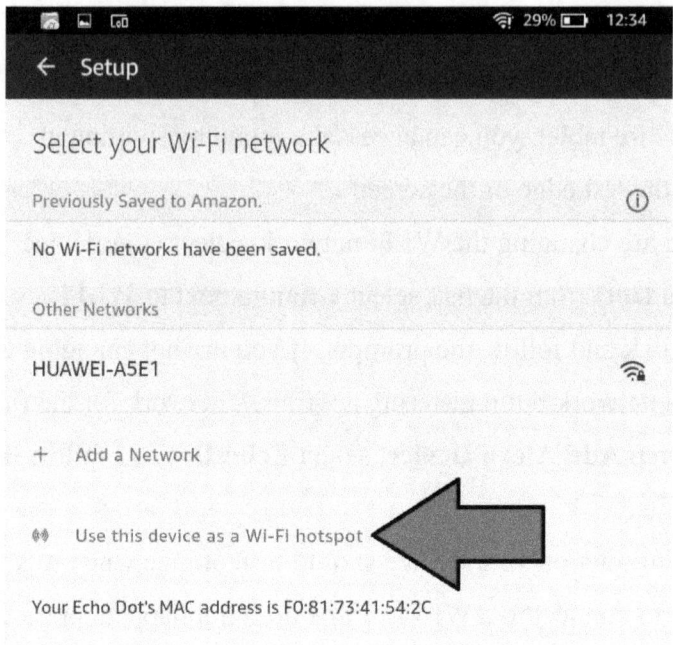

8. After your device connects to your Wi-Fi hotspot network, Alexa should confirm a successful connection.
9. That is all. You can now ask Alexa what you will like it to do.

Change the Wake Word

To get the attention of Echo Dot you will need to say the wake word followed by the command.
Amazon allows you to choose between Alexa, Computer, Echo, or Amazon

To change your wake word:
1. While the Echo Dot is connected to a power source and working, open the Alexa app on your mobile device.

2. In the Alexa app, tap the menu button ☰ located at the top left corner of the screen, then tap **Alexa Devices**. If you are using Fire tablet, you can access the menu by swiping in from the left edge of the screen.
3. Select your device (Echo Dot) from the menu.
4. Scroll down and select **Wake Word**.

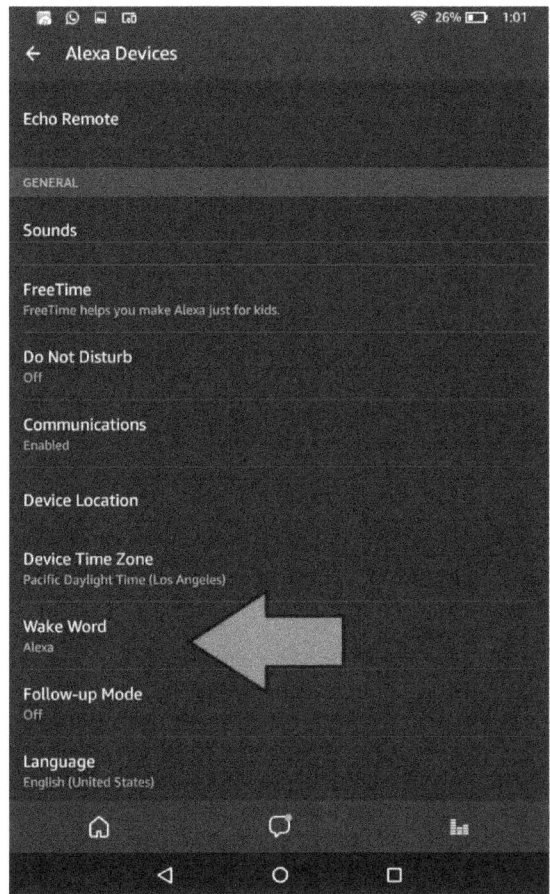

5. Tap the drop-down menu to select a wake word and tap **Ok/Save**. When you change the wake word, the light ring on

13

your device should flash orange briefly. Also, your Echo Dot may be restarted after changing the wake word.
6. Say your new wake word followed by a command to test if everything is ok.

Tip: If you have more than one Alexa devices in your home and you don't want confusion when saying a wake word, use different wake words for the Alexa devices.

In addition, you can change the wake word using your voice. To do this, say **Alexa, change the wake word.**

More importantly, please be careful how you use the wake up. I once read that Amazon Alexa recorded and sent private chat to someone in a contact list. The best thing to do to make sure Alexa don't listen to your private chats is to avoid using the wake word when you don't intend to call the attention of Alexa. Better still, you can turn off the ***microphone*** *(see page 2) whenever you don't want Alexa to respond to wake words.*

Connecting Echo Dot to Bluetooth Devices

Interestingly, Echo Dot is Bluetooth enabled meaning that you can connect it to other Bluetooth enabled devices like your phone or external speaker.

If after following steps mentioned in this guide you are not able to connect an external Speaker to your Echo Dot, it may be that the speaker is not supported. You can check out the list of certified Bluetooth speakers for Echo Dot (3rd Generation) here **https://www.amazon.com/b?node=14048078011**.

In addition, Echo Dot can be connected to an external speaker using 3.5 mm audio cable that is sold separately.

Connecting Echo Dot to a Mobile Bluetooth Device

You can connect Echo Dot to mobile devices like phones and tablets. In this case, your Echo Dot will be acting as external speaker. However, please note that Alexa doesn't receive or read phone calls, text messages, and other notifications from your mobile device.

To connect your Echo Dot to a Bluetooth enabled mobile device:

1. While the Echo Dot is connected to a power source and working, open the Alexa app on your mobile device.
2. In the Alexa app, tap the menu button ☰ located at the top left corner of the screen, then tap **Alexa Devices**. If you are using Fire tablet, you can access the menu by swiping in from the left edge of the screen.
3. Select your Echo Dot from the list and select **Bluetooth/Bluetooth Devices.**
4. Tap **Pair a New Device**. Your Echo Dot then enters pairing mode.

5. On your mobile device, navigate to Bluetooth settings, and select your **Echo Dot**. If you don't see Echo Dot in the list, try scanning for new devices.
6. On your Alexa app screen, tap the name of the device you are trying to connect (if needed). Alexa should then tell you if the connection is established
7. To disconnect your mobile device from Echo Dot, say, **Alexa Disconnect**.
8. To connect to this mobile device again, turn on Bluetooth on your mobile devise and say **Alexa Connect My Mobile Device (or Alexa Pair My Mobile Device)**. Echo Dot will then connect to the device that was last connected.

Please note that you may need to disconnect your Echo Dot from a speaker before you can connect it to another device. Echo Dot may only connect a single device at a time.

You can control the volume of your device by pressing the volume keys (- or + keys) on the Echo Dot. Alternatively, to control the volume you may say **Alexa** followed by a volume number. For example, you may say **Alexa volume 7.** You may also say **Alexa turn up/down the volume** or say **Alexa mute/unmute.**

Tip: To completely unpair a mobile device from Echo Dot, repeat steps 1 to 3 above and tap the small **v** icon next to the device you want to remove. Then select **Forget Device.**

16

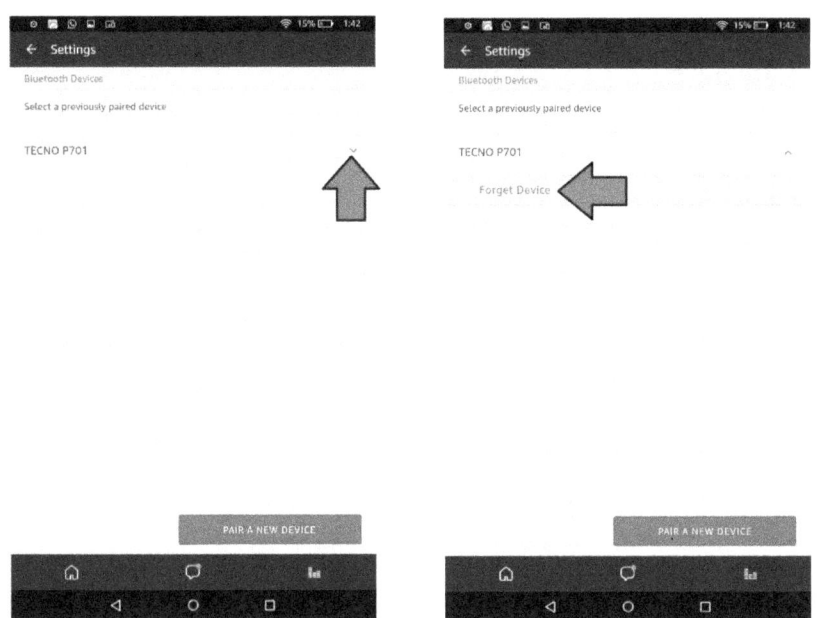

Connecting Echo Dot to a Bluetooth Speaker

You can connect Echo Dot to a Bluetooth speaker. In this case, the Bluetooth speaker will be acting as the external speaker.

To connect Echo Dot to a Bluetooth speaker:

1. Turn on pairing mode on your Bluetooth speaker. You can easily do this by referring to the user guide that came with your Bluetooth speaker.
2. While the Echo Dot is connected to a power source and working, open the Alexa app on your mobile device.
3. In the Alexa app, tap the menu button ☰ located at the top left corner of the screen, then tap **Alexa Devices**.

4. Select your Echo Dot from the list, then select **Bluetooth Devices.**
5. Tap **Pair a New Device**. Your Echo Dot then enters pairing mode.
6. Echo Dot searches for Bluetooth devices. Then the external speaker appears in the list of available of devices in the Alexa app.
7. Select your Bluetooth speaker. You should get a confirmation message from Alexa when your Echo Dot connects to the speaker.
8. To disconnect your speaker from Echo Dot, say, **Alexa Disconnect**.
9. To connect to this speaker again or a previously paired device, say **Alexa Connect My Bluetooth Speaker (or Alexa Pair My Bluetooth Speaker)**. Echo Dot will connect to the device that was last connected.

Tip: To completely disconnect a Bluetooth speaker from Echo Dot, repeat steps 2 to 4 above. Then select the Bluetooth speaker you want to disconnect and select **Forget Device**. To reconnect it again, repeat step 1 to 7 above. Removing and reconnecting a Bluetooth device is a cool way to solve some connections issues.

You can control the volume of your device by pressing the volume keys (- or + keys) on the Echo Dot or the volume the keys on your external speaker. Alternatively, to control the volume you may say **Alexa** followed by a volume number. For example, you may say **Alexa volume 7.** You may also say **Alexa turn up/down the volume** or say **Alexa mute/unmute.**

Using Echo Dot with IFTTT

IFTTT (If This Then That) is an online service that allows you to automate different actions. Although Alexa can perform a lot of tasks, it can't do everything. Connecting your Alexa device to IFTTT allows you to perform some actions that may not be possible with Alexa alone. With the help of IFTTT, Echo Dot can be used to perform actions that are not officially supported.

To connect Echo Dot to IFTTT:
1. From your web browser go to ifttt.com
2. Click on **Sign in**, if you don't have an account click on **Sign up**.
3. Enter the necessary information and click Sign in or Sign up.
4. Click on search button located at the top of the screen.

5. Search for **Amazon Alexa.** The list filters as you type. Click on **Amazon Alexa.**
6. Click on **Connect.**
7. Enter your Amazon login information and click on **Sign In...**

Using IFTTT

After you have connected Amazon Alexa and IFTTT, you will need to choose some applets. Applets are simple conditional statements/actions which are triggered based on what you tell Alexa to do.

For example, you may choose an applet that allows you to receive an email with your complete Shopping list in your Gmail account when you ask Alexa to review your Shopping list. To do this, while on Amazon Alexa channel page, just scroll down, click on the icon shown below, click on **Turn on** and follow the onscreen instructions.

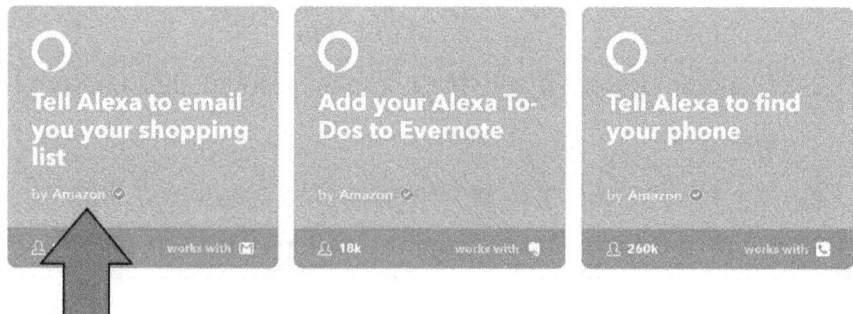

Tip: After activating this recipe, you can get an email of your shopping list just by saying **Alexa, what's on my shopping list?**

Using Echo Dot with Different Types of Skills

You can give a new set of skills to your Echo Dot using the Alexa app. So, what is a skill? A skill is a special action performed by Alexa/Echo Dot when it is connected to another device, app, website or item. For example, you can give Echo Dot some extra mathematical skills by connecting it to a third-party app called **Math Puzzle.** In addition, you can give Echo Dot some flight information capabilities by connecting it to a third-party app called **KAYAK.** Furthermore, you can give Echo Dot some smart control capabilities by connecting it to a skill called **SmartThings**.

In a nutshell, connecting a skill to Echo Dot transforms the way you use this device. It lets you do what you can't do with Echo Dot alone. In this section of the guide, you will be learning the basic steps to follow to connect a new skill to Echo Dot.

To add a skill to Echo Dot:

1. Open Alexa app and tap on the menu icon ☰ located at the top left corner of the screen.
2. Tap on **Skills & Games.**
3. Tap on **Categories** and choose a category and then a skill you like. Alternative, tap the Search bar located at the top of the screen and enter a search phrase.
4. Tap a skill, read the skill descriptions and then tap **Enable** to activate the opened skill. Please note that you may be required to enter some account information to fully enable a skill.

5. You are now ready to use the new skill.

Tip: To link a smart home device, just follow the steps 1 to 3 above and tap on **Smart Home** category. Then choose a skill corresponding to the smart home device you are trying to use with Alexa. Tap **Enable** and follow the prompts. Thereafter, Ask Echo Dot to discover your smart home devices. Simply say, "Discover my devices" and wait for a response to know whether the discovery is completed. That is all, you can begin to control your smart home devices using your Echo Dot.

Please note that it is important you read the **skill description page** to know how to manage a smart home skill/device.

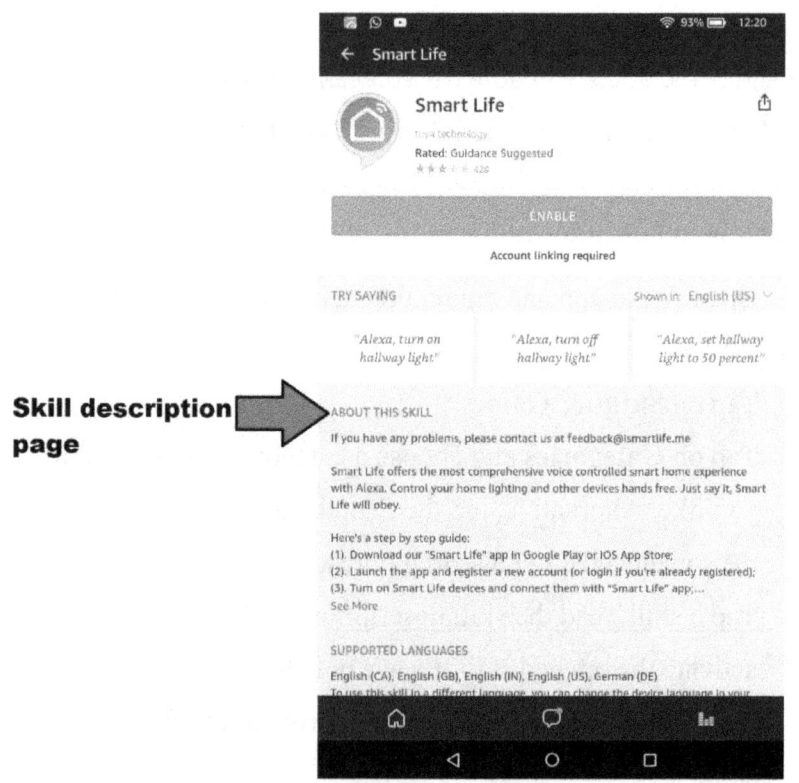

In addition, you may be able to enable/disable some skills using your voice (you have to say their exact name). For example, you may say:

- **Alexa, enable Kayak**
- **Alexa, disable Kayak**

Hint: Do you want to use Echo Dot in a special way? Then add nice Skills to it. You can know how to use a Skill by reading the information on the details page of the Skill.
In addition, you can know the top skills on Amazon by saying, **Alexa, what are your top skills?**

Connecting Your Smart Devices to Echo Dot

You can link many smart home devices by following the steps mentioned on page 21/22. However, it appears that not all smart home devices can be linked by following these aforementioned steps. Some devices require you to have Echo search for them on your network and connect with them. To link those devices that may not require a skill:

1. Open Alexa app and tap on the menu icon ≡ located at the top left corner of the screen.
2. Tap on **Smart Home.**
3. Tap **Devices** and tap on **Discover Devices** or **Add devices**
   You may avoid these first three steps and just tell your Echo

Dot to discover devices connected to your network by saying, **Alexa Discover Devices.**

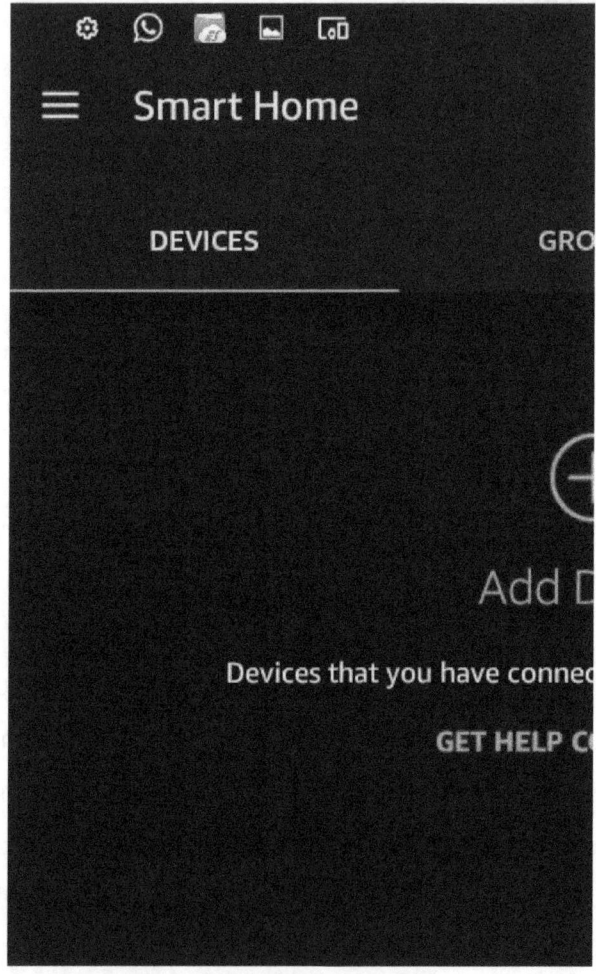

4. Alexa app will then begin scanning your network for any connected smart home devices. In the case of the Philips Hue system, any application or device (including Alexa app) that wants access to the Hue bridge requires you tap the physical button on the Hue bridge to authorize it. So, if you are using

a Philips Hue system, make sure you tap the physical button on the Hue bridge after you say **Alexa, discover devices**.

5. Then you will see the list of all discovered devices on the Alexa app. Tap **Forget/Remove** next to a device's name to prevent Echo Dot from controlling the device or to remove the device. Please note that if a device does not appear under the discovered devices list, it may be that you will need to install the skill for the device instead. To install a skill for a smart home device, please go to page 21/22.

6. You are now ready to use your smart home devices with Echo Dot. But before you do that there is one more important thing to do and that is grouping your devices.

Tip: If after following the steps mentioned in this guide Echo Dot can't still discover your device, check the companion app for your smart home device to ensure that it's on the same Wi-Fi network as your Echo Dot.

To check or change the Wi-Fi network of your Echo Dot/Alexa app:

- Open the Alexa app, tap the menu button ☰ located at the top left corner of the screen, then tap **Alexa devices**. If you are using Fire tablet, you can access the menu by swiping in from the left edge of the screen.
- Select your device **(Echo Dot)** from the list. Select **Change** next to **Wi-Fi Network** and then follow the prompts.

Please note that if you turn off or unplug your smart home device and then turn it back on, it may take some time before Alexa can rediscover the device

Hint: Please note that connecting Echo Dot to your smart home devices could make anyone control your smart home devices by speaking to Echo Dot. To avoid this, I would advise you switch off the **microphone** (see page 2) of your device when not in use. In addition, follow all the safety recommendations suggested by your smart home manufacturer. Furthermore, for security purpose, make sure you confirm an action is completed on your smart home device after making a request.

Grouping Your Smart Home Devices

Grouping your smart home devices allow you to control Echo Dot smartly. For example, you can create a group and name it **bedroom light** so that Echo Dot can access them whenever you make a command and you include bedroom light in the command. Please note that Echo Dot may not recognize any group you have created on your smart home device and you may need to create new groups using Alexa app.

To create a group:
1. Open Alexa app and tap on the menu icon ≡ located at the top left corner of the screen.
2. Tap on **Smart Home**
3. Select **Groups.**
4. Tap **Add Group.**

5. If needed, select **Smart Home Group**.
6. Enter the group name in the field provided. Give your group a recognizable name for Alexa to recognize. For example, you may use the name **Living Room light** to denote the light bulbs in your living room. It is advisable to use unique name for each group but avoid using names with many syllables. In addition, if you have multiple groups, avoid starting the name of the groups with the same first word. For example, **living room bulbs** and **living room small bulbs** are too similar.
7. Select the smart home device(s) you want to add to the group, and then tap **Add/Save**.

Note: Please note that you might need to add smart home device(s) before you could create a group.

To edit/manage a group:

1. Open Alexa app and tap on the menu icon ☰ located at the top left corner of the screen.
2. Tap on **Smart Home**
3. Under **Groups**, select your smart home group.
4. Make the necessary changes by tapping the required field.

Troubleshooting Skills

If you find out that a skill is not working properly or a responding, you may try any of these:

1. Open the Alexa app, tap the menu button ☰ located at the top left corner of the screen and then tap **Skills & Games**.
2. Tap **Your Skills** (located at the top of the screen).

3. Locate the skill in question and tap it to go to detail page.
4. Select **Disable Skill** and follow the prompts.
5. Re-enable the skill again.
6. Restart Echo Dot and then try using the skill again.

If the steps above do not solve the problem, then try:
1. Repeat step 1 to 3 above.
2. Check whether there is **Skill Permissions** page on the detail page. If there is Skill Permissions page, then tap **Manage Permissions**. Thereafter, use the indicator switch to turn on or off permissions.
3. Restart Echo Dot and then try using the skill again.

Communicating with Echo Dot

Speaking to Echo Dot

One of the ways you will interact with Echo Dot is by saying your questions. To get Echo Dot into action, you would need to get its attention. To do that, say the wake word followed by a command e.g. **Alexa, what is on my calendar today.**

Tip: If you wish, you can get the Echo Dot to repeat an answer. To do this, simply say "Alexa, can you repeat that?" and it should.

Getting What You Want from Echo Dot

There are many things you can ask Echo Dot to do for you and before you finish reading this guide you will learn how to effectively interact with it.

I will like to mention that interacting with Echo Dot is not an examination (so there is nothing like cheating) and you get help by saying **Alexa, what can you do**?

Using Echo Dot with Smart Home Devices

You can use Echo Dot to control your smart home devices. This is particularly interesting; imagine telling Alexa to turn on/off the light with just a voice command.

I will assume that you have already connected your smart home devices to your Echo Dot using the instructions mentioned on page 23.

After connecting your smart home device to Echo Dot, then try any of these example commands:

- Alexa, turn on/off (smart home device/group name). For example, you may say **Alexa, turn off bedroom light**.
- Alexa, brighten/dim (smart home device/group name). For example, you may say **Alexa, brighten my living room light.** You may also say **Alexa, set my living room light to maximum**.
- Alexa set (smart home device/group name) temperature to (lower/higher) degrees. For example, you may say **Alexa, set Samsung thermostat to 20 degrees.**
- Alexa, set (smart home device/group name) to "x". For example, you may say **Alexa, set living room fan to 5.**

Note: As I have said before, you will need to connect your smart home devices to your Echo Dot before you can use your Echo Dot to control these devices. To learn how to connect your Echo Dot to your smart device, please go to page 23.

Tip: Some smart home skills may support other device actions. To know what actions is supported go to the smart home skill in the Alexa app. To do this:

1. Open Alexa app and tap on the menu icon ☰ located at the top left corner of the screen.
2. Tap on **Skills & Games**.
3. Tap on **Categories** and tap **Smart Home.** Then read the descriptions under each skill.

Using Quick Commands (Routines) to Manage Echo Dot Like a Pro

Quick commands (routines) allow you to use Echo Dot in a special way. When you say a specific quick command, you trigger a set of actions from Alexa.

Examples of quick commands include:

a) Alexa Start my day b) Alexa, Goodnight c) Alexa, on my way d) Alexa, Driving.

For example, if you say **Alexa, Goodnight**, a set of actions (attached to Goodnight) are performed by Echo Dot.

To enable and manage quick commands (routines):

1. Open Alexa app and tap on the menu icon ☰ located at the top left corner of the screen.
2. Tap on **Routines**. Alternatively, tap on **Settings**, then **Routines**.
3. Tap the plus icon next to **Create Routine**.

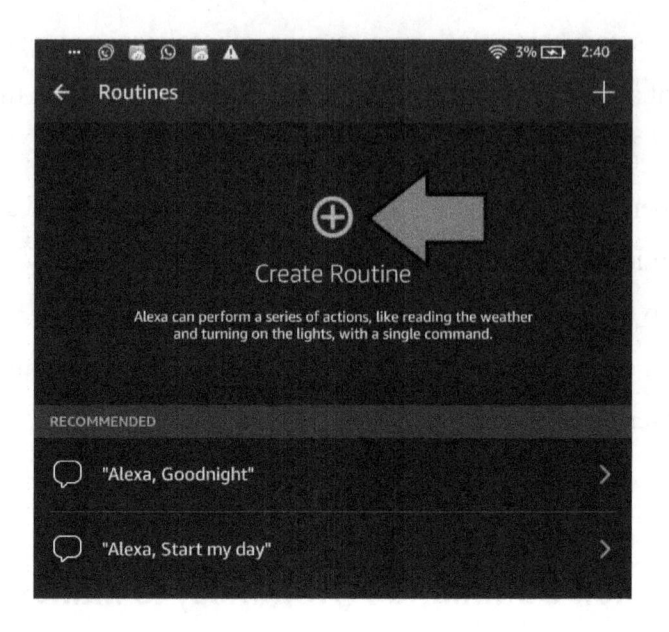

4. Tap **When this happens**. Then tap **Voice**. Type in an example command, for example, type in **shut down**.
5. Tap **Add action**. Tap a category and select a sub-category if needed. Then select **Add**.
6. To add another action, select **Add action**. Tap a category and select a sub-category if needed. Then select **Add**.
7. To remove an action, tap the minus icon next to the action.

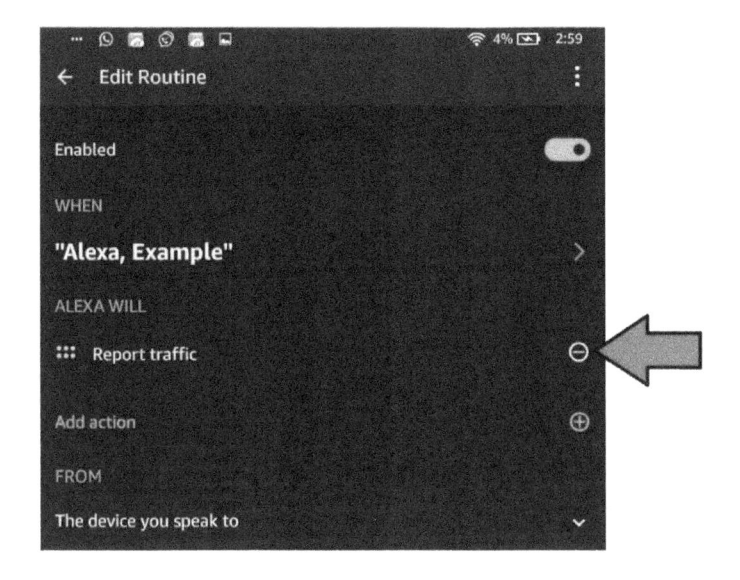

8. Tap **Create** and wait for the process to finish.
9. To add more quick commands, tap the plus icon + at the top of the screen and repeat steps 4 to 8 above.

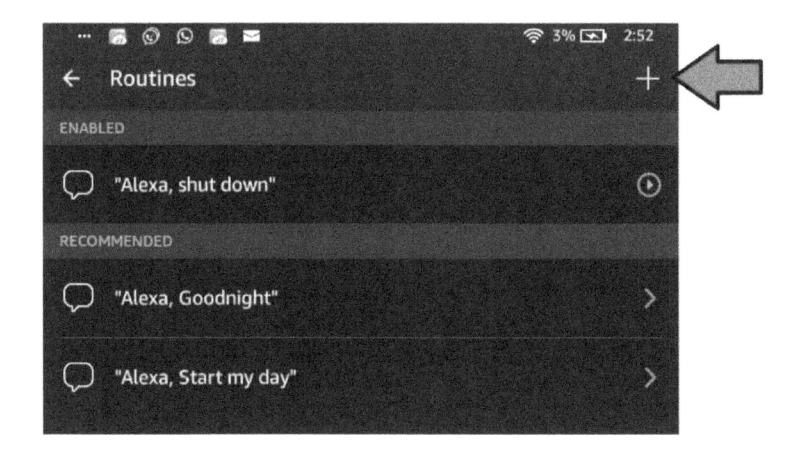

10. To delete a quick command (routine), tap the routine, and tap the menu icon located at the top of the screen. Then select **Delete Routine**.

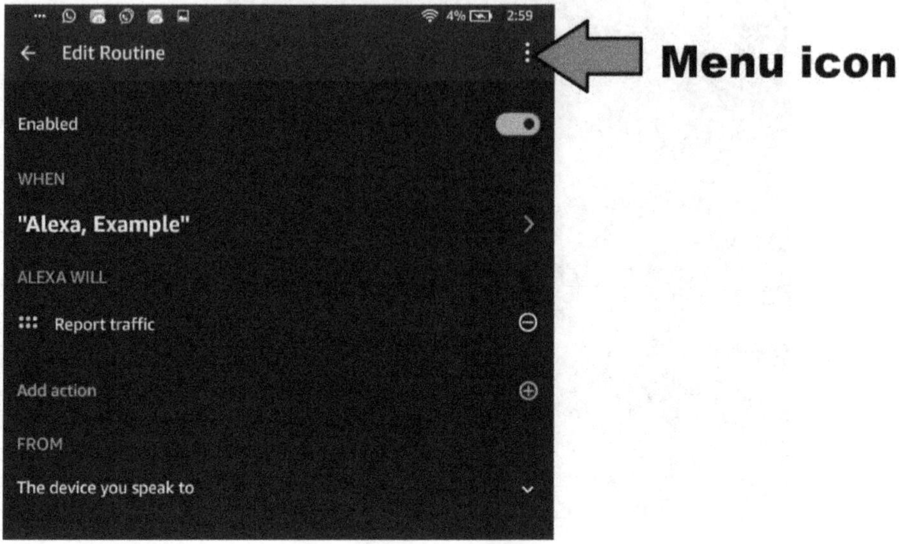

That is all! Now you can get Alexa to perform all the chosen actions by saying your quick command.

Tip: You could add more actions to a quick command. To do this, tap the quick command and select **Add action**. Then follow the prompts.

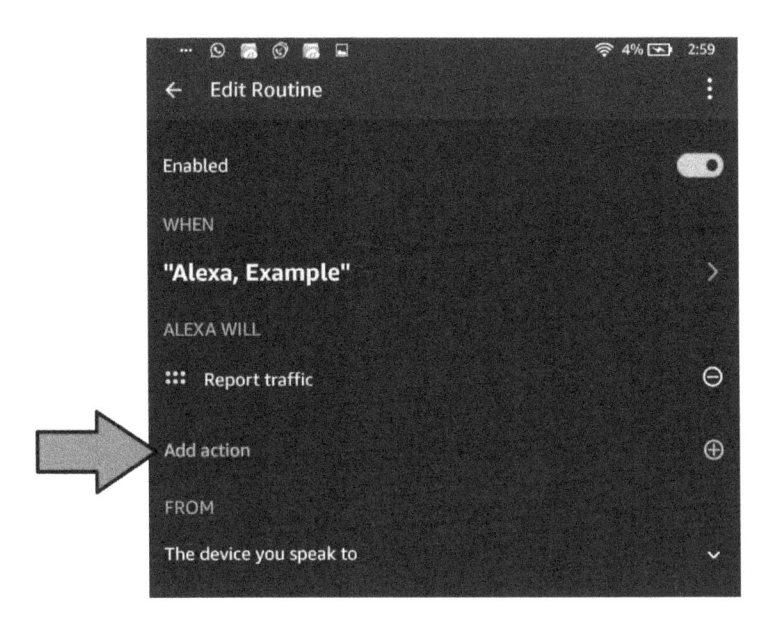

Using Echo Dot with Your Calendar

One of the fantastic features that Echo Dot can do for you is making an appointment.

With just few commands you can get Echo Dot to put an event or appointment into your calendar. But before you can populate your calendar with events, you will need to first link your calendar with your Echo Dot. To do this:

Please note that you may need to setup a calendar account before you can complete the steps mentioned below. You can setup a Google calendar by visiting **https://calendar.google.com**

1. Open Alexa app and tap on the menu icon ☰ located at the top left corner of the screen.
2. Tap on **Settings**
3. Scroll down and tap on **Calendar** and select an account and follow the prompts.
4. To unlink your calendar at a future time, tap the account type and tap **Unlink this…**

After linking your Calendar to Echo Dot, you may try the following commands.

- **Alexa, what is on my calendar tomorrow?**
- **Alexa add an event to my calendar.**
- **Alexa, how does my calendar look like today**?
- **Alexa, add meeting with Clinton to my calendar for Friday at 6 a.m.**
- **Alexa add an appointment with Steve for Monday at 1 p.m.**

Please note that you can also say all the examples given above in other ways, the most important thing is to get Echo Dot to understand what you are saying.

Using Echo Dot with Your Shopping List and To-do List

There are probably many things going through your mind and it will be quite interesting if you can get a personal assistant to assist in putting it down inside a list. Fortunately, Echo Dot can help you in this regard.

To add an item to your to-do list or shopping list, try any of the following commands:

- **Alexa, add 'go to my in-law's house' to my to-do list**
- **Alexa, add (item) to my shopping list**
- **Alexa, what's on my shopping list**
- **Alexa, what's on my to-do List?**

Hint: To empty your to-do list, say **Alexa, clear my to-do list** or say **Alexa, clear my shopping list**. To remove a specific item from your list, say **Alexa, remove [item's name] from my shopping/to-do list**.

In addition, if your Echo Dot is not nearby and you want to manage your shopping or to-do list, all you have to do is to:

1. Open Alexa app and tap on the menu icon located at the top left corner of the screen.
2. Tap on **Lists**.
3. Select either **Shopping** or **To-do**.

4. To add a new item to the list, tap the plus icon "+ **Add Item**". Then enter the name of the item and tap the done (or new line) button on the virtual keyboard of your phone or tablet.

In addition, you can print your list if you are accessing Alexa from a computer, to access Alexa from a computer, go to http://alexa.amazon.com. Then in the left navigation menu click **Lists.** Choose either **Shopping** or **To-do**. Then select **Print**.

Using Echo Dot with Alarm

You can also set an alarm using this personal assistant. To do this, try these example commands:

- **Alexa, set an alarm for 1 p.m. tomorrow**
- **Alexa, set an alarm for 30 minutes from now.**

Tip: To stop the alarm when it is sounding, say **Alexa, stop the alarm**. You may also say **Alexa, snooze the alarm.** This will snooze the alarm for a particular period of time.

To set a repeating alarm, try this:

- **Alexa, set an everyday alarm for 7 a.m.**

To know the status of your alarm, try these:

- **Alexa, what time is my alarm set for?**
- **Alexa, what alarms do I have for Monday?**

To edit/delete an alarm use the Alexa app. To do this:

1. Open Alexa app and tap on the menu icon ☰ located at the top left corner of the screen.
2. Tap on **Reminders & Alarms**.
3. Choose your device by tapping the dropdown menu.

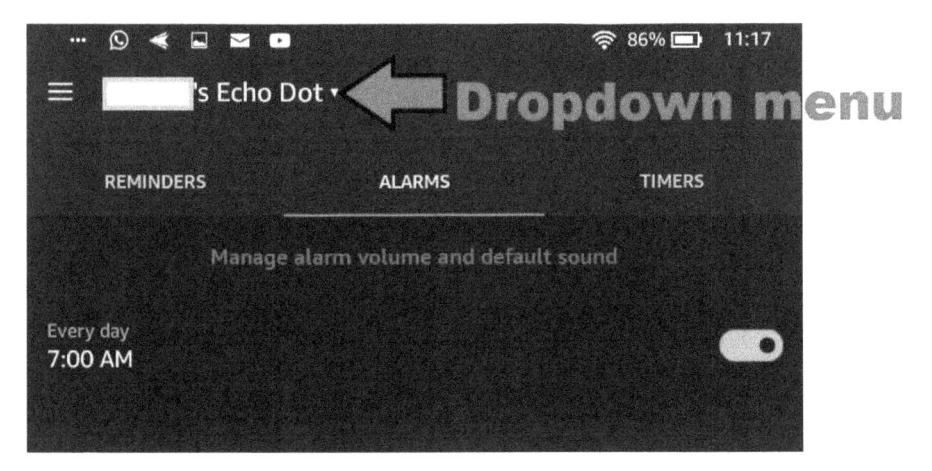

4. Select the **Alarms** tab.
5. To edit an alarm, tap the alarm. Tap **Time** and adjust it as you like. Then tap **Save** located at the top of the screen to save changes.
6. To delete an alarm, tap the alarm you want to delete, and then select **Delete alarm**.

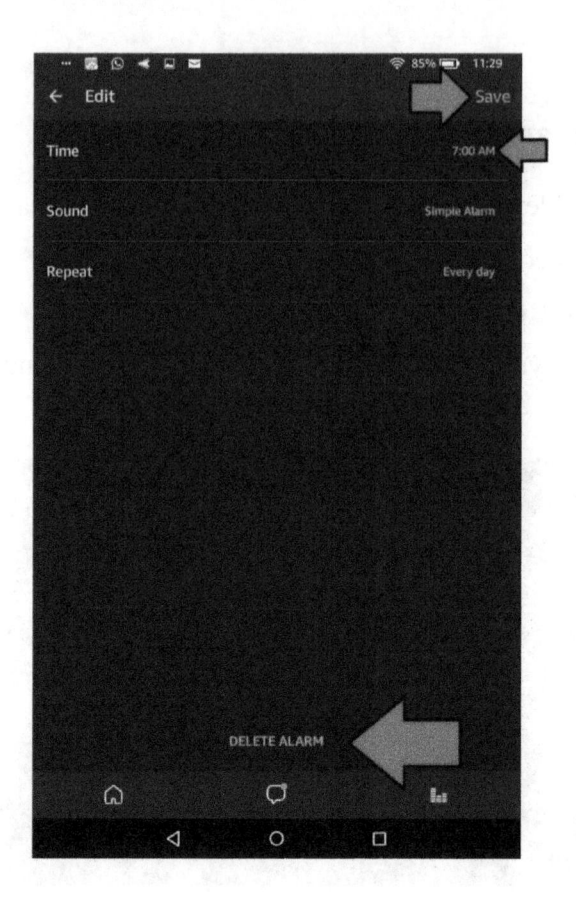

To change your alarm volume/sound:

1. Repeat steps 1 to 4 above.
2. Tap **Manage alarm volume and default sound**.

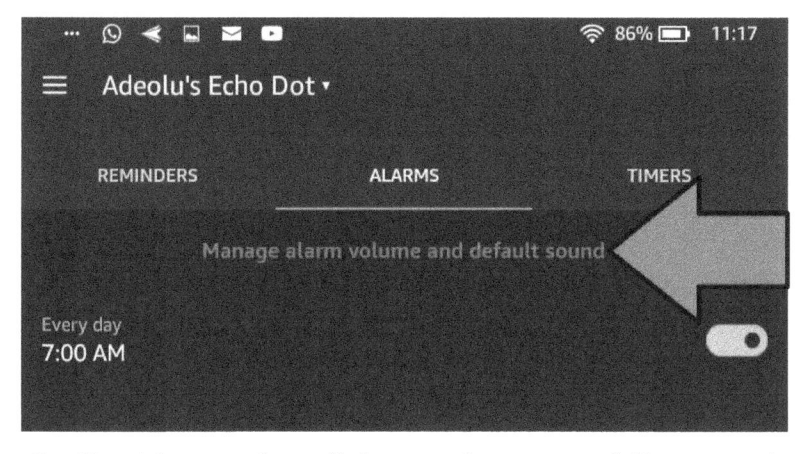

3. Tap **Alarm** and scroll down and tap a sound. For example, you may select **Countertop**.
4. To adjust the alarm's volume, adjust the volume's slider to the level you want.

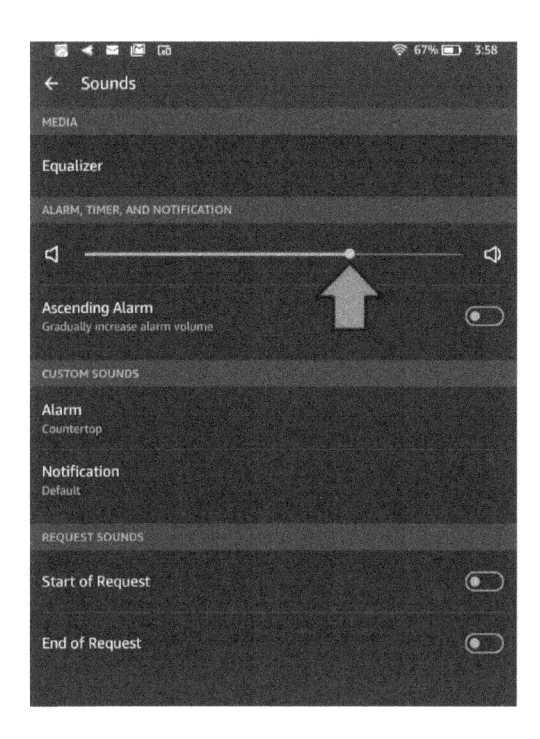

5. Tap the back arrow ⬅ located at the top of the screen to save the changes.

Tip: To adjust the alarm sound for a specific alarm, repeat step 1 above and then tap an alarm. Tap sound, scroll down and tap a sound. For example, you may select **Countertop**. Tap the back arrow ⬅ located at the top of the screen and then tap **Save** to save the changes

Using Echo Dot with Timer

You can set a timer using this personal assistant. To do this, try these example commands:

- **Alexa, set a timer for 30 minutes.**
- **Alexa, set a timer for 3 p.m.**

Tip: To stop the timer when it is sounding, say **Alexa, stop the timer**.

To know the status of your timer, try this:

- **Alexa, how much time is left on my timer?**

To manage a timer:

1. Open Alexa app and tap on the menu icon ☰ located at the top left corner of the screen.
2. Tap on **Reminders & Alarms.**

3. Choose your device by tapping the dropdown menu.

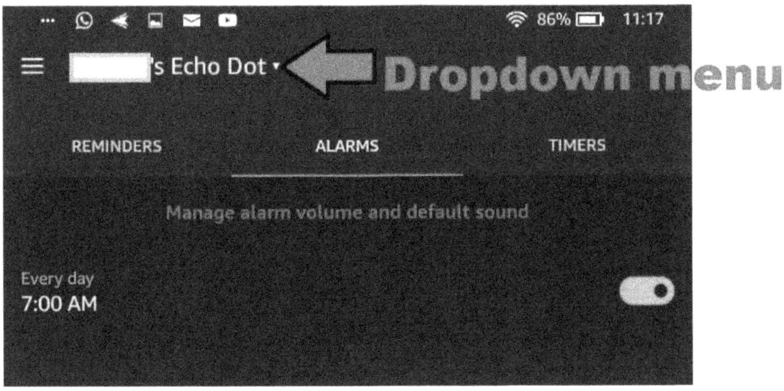
86%
11:17
's Echo Dot
Dropdown menu
REMINDERS
ALARMS
TIMERS
Manage alarm volume and default sound
Every day
7:00 AM

4. Select the **Timers** tab.
5. To edit a timer, tap the timer. Tap **Pause** to pause the timer.
6. To delete a timer, tap **Delete Timer**.

Tip: You can also use your voice to delete an upcoming timer; just say **Alexa cancel the timer for (amount of time).**

To change your timer volume:

1. Repeat steps 1 to 4 above.
2. Tap **Manage timer volume.**
3. Tap and drag the volume bar for **Alarm, Timer and Notification**.

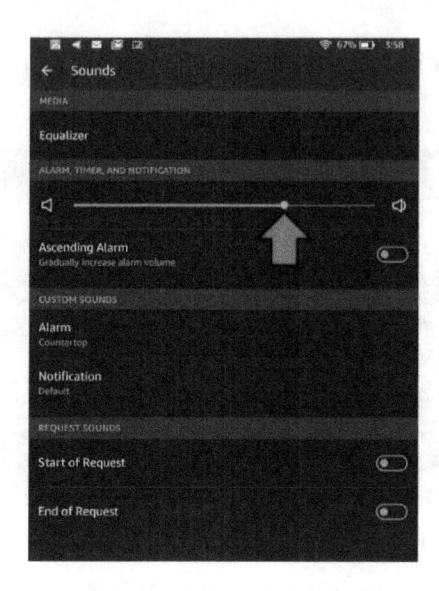

Using Echo Dot with Clock

You can ask Echo Dot what your local time is. In addition, it can also tell you the time in a specific place. To do this, try these example commands:

- **Alexa what is the time?**
- **Alexa what is the time in New York?**

Using Echo Dot to Get Flight Information

You can also use this personal assistant to get information about a flight. This is a smarter way to know when a particular airplane will take off.

To do this, try these example command:

- **Alexa, what is the flight status of Delta 400?**

To have more robust management of flight information, you may need to connect Echo Dot to a skill called **Kayak.** To do this:

1. Open Alexa app and tap on the menu icon ☰ located at the top left corner of the screen.
2. Tap on **Skills & Games**
3. Type **Kayak** into the search bar located at the top of the screen.
4. Tap **Kayak** and follow the onscreen instructions to link this skill to Echo Dot.

That is it; you have now given your Echo Dot some new capabilities. Now you can ask Alexa some flight related questions like:

Alexa ask Kayak how much it costs to fly from New York to Seattle?

Tip: You might also enable Kayak by saying **Alexa, enable Kayak.**

Listen to Your Audiobooks

Alexa can read audiobooks to you.

To read an audiobook you own, try any of these:
- **Alexa, read (title)**
- **Alexa, play the book, (title)**
- **Alexa, read the audiobook, (title)**

To pause an audiobook, simply say **Alexa, Pause.** To resume, say **Alexa, resume my audiobook.**

To go back or forward in the audiobook by 30 seconds, say **Alexa, go back/forward**

To go to the next or previous chapter in an audiobook, say **Alexa, next chapter** or **Alexa, previous chapter**.

Say **Alexa, go to chapter 2** to go to a specific chapter.

To stop reading in a future time, say **Alexa stop reading the book in (x) minutes/hours.** Where x represents a number.

Read Kindle Books with Alexa

Alexa can read eligible Kindle books using text-to-speech technology.

To read a Kindle book you own, try any of these:

- **Alexa, read my Kindle book (title)**
- **Alexa, play the book (title)**
- **Alexa, read my book (title)**

To pause a Kindle book, simply say **Alexa, Pause.** To resume, say **Alexa, resume my Kindle book.**

To go next or previous paragraph in a Kindle book, say **Alexa, go back/forward**

Buying Items Using Your Voice

You can talk to Echo Dot to order an item for you. To do this, you will first need to

1. Open Alexa app and tap on the menu icon ☰ located at the top left corner of the screen.
2. Tap on **Settings**.
3. Scroll down and tap **Voice Purchasing**.
4. Tap an option:
    a. **Purchase by voice**: Use the option to enable or disable voice purchasing
    b. **(Optional) Voice Code:** This option allows you to enter a 4-digit code which Alexa will ask for before you complete a purchase.
    c. **View 1-Click settings**: Use this option to update your 1-Click payment method. 1-Click payment method is required for voice purchasing.

After this setup, you may shop for products on Amazon using your voice. To order a product, you may say:

Alexa, order me (item name)

To reorder an item say **Alexa, reorder (item name)**

Please note that when ordering an item, you Alexa may ask you some questions, simply follow the voice prompts.

To cancel an order immediately after placing it, say **Alexa, cancel my order**.

To add an item to your cart on Amazon, say **Alexa, add (item name) to my cart.**

To track your orders, say **Alexa, track my order** or say **Alexa, where is my stuff?**

Tip: To better manage your orders or contact a seller, go to amazon website. In addition, to manage your shopping notifications, while in Alexa app, click on the menu icon ☰ and select **Settings**. Then tap on **Notifications**, then **Shopping Notifications**.

Using Echo Dot to Get Traffic Information

You can use the Echo Dot to get information about traffic situation on your route. To get this you will first need to tell Alexa what your route is. To do this:

1. Open Alexa app and tap on the menu icon ☰ located at the top left corner of the screen.
2. Tap on **Settings**.
3. Select **Traffic**.
4. Enter your starting point and destination in the **From** and **To** sections by selecting **Change address**.
5. Tap **Save changes**.

After this setup, you can get traffic information about your route by asking Alexa questions like:

- **Alexa, what's my commute?**
- **Alexa, what's traffic like right now?**
- **Alexa, how is my traffic?**

What about Math?

Echo Dot can also help you with some mathematics and conversions. For example, you can tell Echo Dot "**Alexa, what is the square root of four?**" You may also say "**Alexa, how many centimeters are in one foot?**" or "**Alexa, what is 60 factorial**?" and so on.

Please note that you can say all the examples given above in other ways, the most important thing is to get Echo Dot to understand what you are saying.

Using Echo Dot to get definitions

You can quickly check for a meaning of a word by asking Echo Dot. For example, you may say "**Alexa, what is the meaning of flabbergasted?**"

Using Echo Dot with Wikipedia

You can use Echo Dot to get information from Wikipedia.
To get Wikipedia information, say **Alexa, Wikipedia [subject]**.

Using Echo to Listen to Radio Programs

Echo can work with internet radio service providers like TuneIn.

To start listening to radio station straightaway, you may say:

- **Alexa, play (radio station) on TuneIn.**

Using Echo Dot to Get Flash Briefing

You can use Amazon Echo Dot to get news briefing, to do this:

1. Open Alexa app and tap on the menu icon ☰ located at the top left corner of the screen.
2. Tap on **Settings**.
3. Scroll down (if needed) and select **Flash Briefing** and then use the switch next to each item to select what you want.
4. To get more flash briefing content, tap on **Get more Flash Briefing content**. Then select a skill and enable it. To return to the settings page, tap the back button.
5. To arrange how programs play in your Flash Briefing, tap **Edit Order** (located at the upper right part of the screen). Then tap and drag the three lines icon ≡ next to an item on the list to move it to a new location. Tap **Done** (located at the top right part of the screen) to save the changes.

After this setup, you can then hear your flash briefing using Echo Dot. To hear your flash briefing, you may say:

Alexa, what's my Flash Briefing?
Alexa, what's new?
To go back to the previous/next news, say **Alexa, previous/next.**
To stop the flash briefing, say **Alexa, stop.**

Using Echo Dot to Get General Information

If you will like to know more about something you can ask Echo Dot. For example, you may say **Alexa, what is the shape of the earth?**

Using Echo Dot to Make an Announcements or Broadcast

If you have two or more Alexa devices connected to your account, you could broadcast a message on all them at once. You can think of this as a one-way intercom. To do this:

Say **Alexa, announce [your message]**. You could also say, **Alexa, broadcast [your message]** or **Alexa, tell everyone [your message]**.

Tip: You could get Alexa to broadcast a message on your family members' Alexa devices by setting up Amazon household. To set up a household, while in Alexa app, click on the menu icon ☰ and select **Settings**. Scroll down and tap **Household Profile**. Carefully read the onscreen instruction, click on **Start** and follow the prompts.

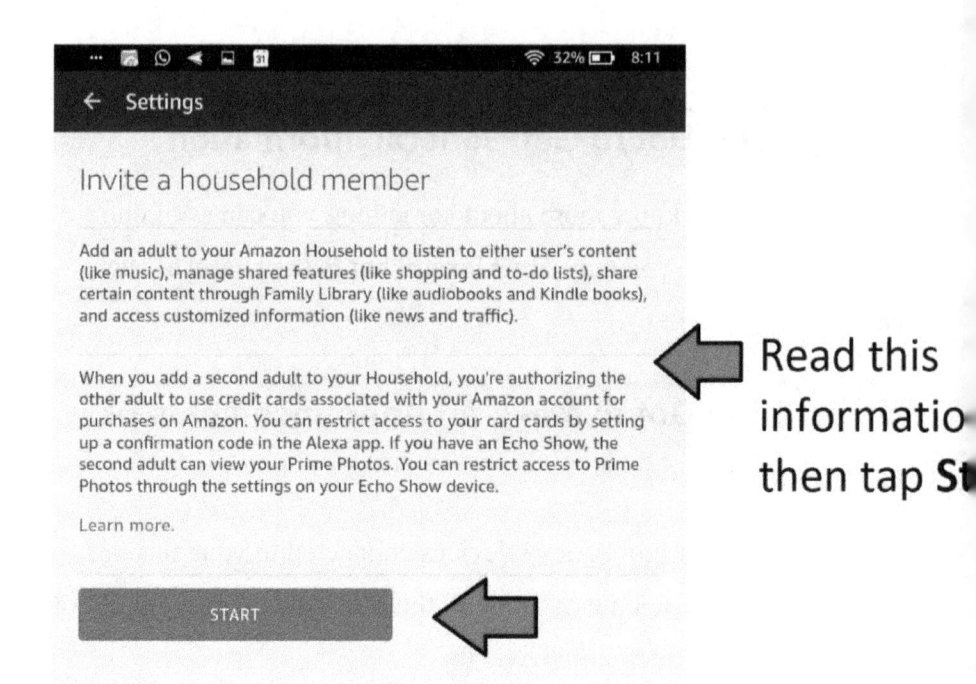

Tip: Echo Dot can repeat what you have said. To do this, simply say **Alexa, Simon says** [then mention what you want Echo Dot to say].

Funny sides of Echo Dot

One of the main features that that makes Echo Dot interesting is its ability to give a reply in funny manner. This all depends on what you ask it. Some of the questions you can ask it to get funny replies are given below:

- **Alexa, do you sleep?**

- **Alexa, do you eat?**

- **Alexa, do you like your job?**

- **Alexa, do you have a brain?**

- **Alexa, are you lying?**

The list of questions you can ask Echo Dot to get funny replies goes on like that. As I have said before, it all depends on the type of question you ask this device.

Calling and Messaging on Echo Dot

You can call, and message supported devices using your Echo Dot. To get started, you may need to sign up for Alexa calling.

Signing up for Alexa Calling
1. Open the Alexa app.
2. Tap the conversation icon 💬 located at the bottom of the screen.
3. Fill in your name and tap **Continue**
4. Verify your phone number and tap **Continue**. Then wait for the process to complete.

Using Alexa Drop In

Drop In feature allows you to drop in on your contacts and connected Alexa devices. Drop In is different from voice call in that you get automatically connected to contact (or Alexa devices) you drop in on. This means the contact don't need to manually answer your call. When you use the Drop In feature, you should begin to immediately hear anything near the microphone of the device you are dropping in on.

To drop in on a contact, you have to manually add the contact. In addition, the contact has to allow your Drop In request.

Furthermore, if you use an Alexa device with screen to drop in on another Alexa device with screen, you should be automatically connected to a video chat. To switch off the video option, simply say **Video Off**.

Using and managing Drop In feature

Please note that you would need to sign up for Alexa calling before using the **Drop In** feature. Please see **Signing up for Alexa Calling** to know how to sign up for Alexa Calling.

To use and manage Drop In feature:

1. Open Alexa app and tap the conversation icon . Alternatively, tap on **Set Up Drop In** and follow the prompts.
2. To allow a contact to drop in, click on the contact icon (located at the top of the screen) and select a contact. Then select status switch next to **Contact can Drop In Anytime**.
3. To revoke a Drop In permission for a contact, click on the contact icon. Then select the status switch next to **Contact can Drop In Anytime**.
4. To edit your Alexa contacts, simply do so using the local contact app on your phone/tablet. Alexa should automatically sync with the changes made. Contacts from your Address book who also use Alexa Calling & Messaging should automatically appear in the contacts list in your Alexa app.
5. To use your Echo Dot to drop in, say Alexa, Drop in on [device's name]. To end the Drop In, say **Alexa, hang up**. *Please note that you can't drop in on Alexa app, but you can use Alexa app to drop in on other Alexa devices.*
6. To use Alexa app to drop in, tap the Drop In icon and select the name of the device you want to drop in on. Alternatively, select a contact and tap the Drop In icon. To

55

end the Drop In, tap the screen and select Hang Up (red) button.

Using Echo Dot to Make Calls

You can use Echo Dot to call mobile and landline numbers and other supported Alexa devices.

Please note that you would need to sign up for Alexa Calling before you can make calls. Please see **Signing up for Alexa Calling** to know how to sign up for Alexa Calling.

To make, end and manage a call:

1. To call a supported Alexa device, say **Alexa, call [name of the Alexa device]**.
2. To call a mobile/landline number you don't have its details in your phonebook, say, **Alexa, call [mobile/landline number]**. If you have the contact, say **Alexa call [contact's name]**. You could also say, **Alexa, call [contact's name] on his home phone**.
3. To answer a call, say **Answer**. To ignore a call, say **Ignore**.
4. To reduce or increase the volume, say **Alexa, turn the volume up/down**.
5. To end a call, say **Alexa, hang up**.

Note: Alexa Calling does not support calls to all types of numbers. For example, you may not be able to call some international numbers using Alexa calling.

Sending and Receiving Messages on Echo Dot

You can send message to others supported Alexa devices using your voice or Alexa app. To do this:

1. Say **Alexa, send a message to [device name or contact's name]**. Alexa would then prompt you for the message. Follow the voice prompts to complete the process.

2. To use Alexa app to send a message, open Alexa app and tap the conversation icon . Tap the contact icon located at the top of the screen (if needed). Select a contact from the contact list. Then tap the message icon to start a conversation.

3. When you receive a message, a pulsing yellow light (a yellow light appearing and disappearing) appears. Simply say, **Alexa, play my messages** to listen to your messages.

Using Do Not Disturb

If you don't want to receive alert for calls, messages or Drop In, I would advise you enable Do Not Disturb.

To do this:

1. Open Alexa app and tap on the menu icon located at the top left corner of the screen.
2. Tap on **Alexa Devices**.
3. Select your Echo Dot from the list.
4. Tap **Do Not Disturb**.
5. Tap the status switch next to **Do Not Disturb**.

6. To schedule a time for Do Not Disturb, tap the switch next to **Scheduled** and set the start and end time.

Echo Dot's Settings

The settings tab under Alexa app allows you to manage Echo Dot's functions. To access Alexa settings:

1. Open Alexa app and tap on the menu icon ▤ located at the top left corner of the screen.
2. Tap on **Settings**
3. Tap an option.

Tip: Settings allows to customize your Echo Dot in a special way. Whenever you think of giving your Echo Dot a special tweak, go to settings.

Clearing your voice input and interactions

You could also manage your voice recordings by doing these:

i. Open Alexa app and tap on the menu icon ▤ located at the top left corner of the screen.
ii. Tap on **Settings**.
iii. Tap **Alexa Privacy**.
iv. Tap on **Review Voice History**.
v. Tap the drop-down box next to **Date Range** and select **All History**.
vi. Then select **Delete All Recording for All Time**.

You could also manage smart home history and skill permissions under the **Alexa Privacy** tab.

Tip: You can clear your voice input stored on Alexa using the Amazon website. To do this:

1. Open a web browser and go to **www.amazon.com/mycd**
2. Tap **Your Devices** tab.
3. Tap then three dots icon next to your Echo Dot.

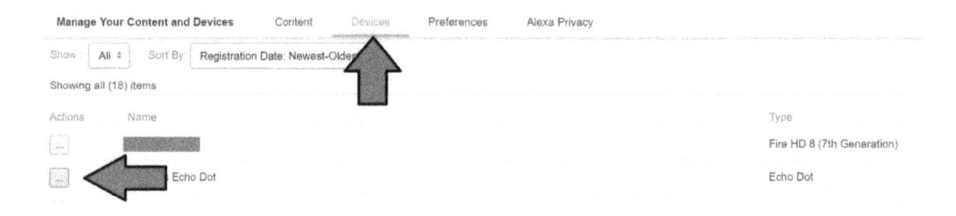

4. Select **Manage Voice recordings**.
5. Select **Delete**.

Troubleshooting Echo Dot

Although much effort has been put into making this device, it is possible that Echo Dot misbehaves at one time or the other. When this happens, there are few things to do.

- **Ensure that you are connected to a strong network**: If you have bad or no internet connection, Echo Dot may not work properly. Therefore, the first thing to check when Echo Dot starts to misbehave is the internet connection.

- **Speak clearly in a silent place**: Make sure you are speaking clearly and try to avoid background noise. In addition, try to be specific in your commands.

- **Try to Restart Your Echo Dot**: If you find out that all what I have mentioned above does not work, you may try restarting your device. To do this, unplug your device and then plug it back after few seconds.

Resetting Echo Dot

If you have restarted your Echo Dot (by unplugging and plugging it back) but it is still misbehaving, you may try resetting your device. You may also reset your Echo Dot if you want to sell it or give it away. Please note that you will need to re-register it to an Amazon account after you perform a reset.

To reset your Echo Dot (3rd Generation):

- Press and hold the **action button** (the small dot button on your Echo Dot) for about 25 seconds.
- Wait for the light ring to turn off and on again. The light ring then turns orange, and Echo Dot will enter setup mode.
- Open the Alexa app to connect your device to a Wi-Fi network and register it to your Amazon account again. To learn more about setting up Echo Dot, go to page 4.

Bonus Chapter –Being Productive with Echo Dot

Not many of us fully understand how will can put Echo Dot to use in managing our day to day affairs. In this section of the guide we will be looking at ways you can put Echo Dot to more uses and manage some of your activities with this device.

Starting Your Day with Echo Dot

It is always good you start your day with what are important to you. Interestingly, Echo Dot can help you in this regard. With simple voice commands you can tell Echo when you need to be woken up and what you want to do or listen to when you wake up.
For example, you can set an alarm to wake up by 5 a.m. every day. To know how to set an everyday alarm, please go to page 38.
After waking up, you can thank the Almighty God for the gift of the day and then tell Echo Dot to tell you what is on your calendar by saying **Alexa, how does my calendar look like today**?
If you need to add any event to your calendar, simply tell Echo Dot to do so. For example, you may say **Alexa, add meeting with Steve to my calendar for Friday at 6 a.m.**
In addition, you can tell Echo Dot to tell you what is on your to-do list by saying **Alexa, what's on my to-do List?**

If you need to add any reminder you can simply say it. For example, you may say **Alexa, remind me at 6 a.m. to fix my car**. Echo will then try to put this in your to-do list. Unfortunately, Echo may not give you any sound notification when it is time to fix your car. You may need to ask Alexa what is on your to-do list to get what is needed to be done next.

To learn more about to-do list please go to page 37.

In addition, you could set up a quick command to get many actions performed at a time. Please go to page 31 to learn more about quick commands.

Reviewing Your Day with Echo Dot

You can also review your day using Echo Dot. For example, you may ask Echo to tell you what is on your calendar today to see whether you have been able to perform all the tasks on your calendar. In addition, you may ask Echo to tell you what is on your to-do list to see whether you have done what needed to be done. To remove anything from your to-do list, read the **hint** on page 37.

63

Just Before You Go... (Please Read!)

We are in the age of information, and to put it straight, we are in the age of information overload. Many people have lost track of keeping up to date. They are fed up of information and they don't even know what to read and what not to. These set of people love information, but they are overwhelmed by it.

Many of us are suffering from information overload, in fact, a survey by Reuters once found that two-thirds of managers believe that the data deluge has made their jobs less satisfying or hurt their personal relationships. One-third thinks that it has damaged their health. Another survey suggests that most managers think most of the information they receive is useless. So, this means you are not the only one having this problem.

What of if there is a way out. Being an infovore myself, I have realized that we need a holistic approach to solve the problem of information overload. We need to change what we eat, where we read, how we plan our time, the number of hours we read, how we filter what we read and so on, in order to really get over this scourge.

Do you want to get control of your life and be on top of useful information? Then you just need to click and subscribe to my newsletter here at https://tinyletter.com/Pharmlbrahim.

Don't worry I hate spam and you can trust me for your privacy.